FEATHERED FRIENDS

WOODPECKERS

Madison Parker

NorwoodHouse Press

Library of Congress Cataloging-in-Publication Data:

Names: Parker, Madison.
Title: Woodpeckers / Madison Parker.
Description: Buffalo, NY : Norwood House Press, 2025. | Series: Feathered friends | Includes glossary and index.
Identifiers: ISBN 9781684502899 (pbk.) | ISBN 9781684502905 (library bound) | ISBN 9781684502912 (ebook)
Subjects: LCSH: Woodpeckers--Juvenile literature.
Classification: LCC QL696.P56 P375 2025 | DDC 598.7'2--dc23

Published in 2025 by
Norwood House Press
2544 Clinton Street
Buffalo, NY 14224

Designer: Ocean Books
Editor: Kim Thompson

Photo credits: Cover, p. 1 Sourabh Bhart/Shutterstock.com; p. 5 Rainan53/Shutterstock.com; p. 6 Prabodha D Herath/Shutterstock.com; p. 7 Jamil Bin Mat Isa/Shutterstock.com; p. 8 Wildmedia/Shutterstock.com; p. 10 Kluciar Ivan Shutterstock.com; p. 11 Miamia/Shutterstock.com; p. 12 Clipp Day Shutterstock.com; p. 13 Tom Reichner/Shutterstock.com; p. 15 Keno Griffiths/Shutterstock.com; p. 16 Victor Suarez Naranjo/Shutterstock.com; p. 17 TashaBubo/Shutterstock.com; p. 19 Susan Hodgson/Shutterstock.com; p. 21 Barbarajo/Shutterstock.com

Printed in the United States of America

CPSIA compliance information: Batch #CW25NHP: For further information contact Norwood House Press at 1-800-237-9932.

TABLE OF CONTENTS

What Do Woodpeckers Look Like?

Woodpeckers are our feathered friends. Many are black and white. Some have bright red or yellow feathers.

Woodpeckers have **stiff** tail feathers. These help them cling to tree trunks as they **peck**.

They tap on trees
with their strong,
pointed **beaks**.
Woodpecker beaks
are long and sharp.

Where Do Woodpeckers Live?

Woodpeckers live in forests, parks, and **woodlands** across North America, Europe, Asia, and Africa. They **thrive** in areas with plenty of trees.

They make nests by pecking holes in tree trunks. Their nests are cozy and safe for their eggs.

How Do Woodpeckers Grow Up?

Woodpecker eggs are white. Baby woodpeckers **hatch** in about two weeks. After one month, they can fly out to find their own food.

What Do Woodpeckers Eat?

Woodpeckers like to eat ants, beetles, and other insects. They find them by pecking at tree bark.

Their tongues are long and sticky. They use their tongues to catch insects hiding deep inside trees.

Woodpeckers also eat fruits and nuts they find in the forest. They crack open nuts with their strong beaks. Sometimes, they snack on seeds at bird feeders.

What Sounds Do Woodpeckers Make?

Woodpeckers tap loudly on trees with their beaks. This helps them find insects hidden in the bark.

They make a drumming noise by pecking quickly on wood or metal. The sound can be heard from far away.

Woodpeckers call out using short, sharp chirps. The chirps help them talk to other woodpeckers nearby.

Woodpeckers make a loud chattering noise when they feel **threatened**. This warns other birds to stay away.

What Funny Things Can Woodpeckers Do?

Woodpeckers hang upside down on branches. They will sip **nectar** from hummingbird feeders. Their wave-like flying pattern looks funny as they glide between trees.

GLOSSARY

beaks (beeks): horny, pointed jaws on birds; bird bills

hatch (hach): to break out of an egg to be born

nectar (NEK-tur): a sweet liquid produced by the flowering parts of plants

peck (pek): to strike something or pick something up with the beak

stiff (stif): rigid or firm; difficult to bend

threatened (THRE-tuhnd): in danger of being harmed

thrive (thrive): to do well and become strong and successful

woodlands (WUD-landz): areas covered mainly with trees

THINKING QUESTIONS

1. What does a woodpecker look like?

2. What is special about the sounds a woodpecker makes?

3. How does a woodpecker show it is smart?

4. What do woodpeckers eat?

5. Why do you think a woodpecker is a feathered friend?

INDEX

ABOUT THE AUTHOR

Madison Parker spent her childhood in the city of Chicago, Illinois. A farm girl at heart, today she lives in Wisconsin with her husband and four children on a small farm with cows, goats, chickens, and two miniature horses named Harley and David. Her favorite dessert is vanilla frozen custard with rainbow sprinkles, even in the winter.